# How To

# Be Happy

Robert A. Wolfson

Published by:

Fidlar-Doubleday, Inc.

www.how2behappy.com

ISBN 1-932133-54-2

Copyright © 2003 Robert A. Wolfson

All rights reserved.

No part of this book may be reproduced without the permission of the publisher.

Fidlar-Doubleday, Inc.

# Table Of Contents

Dedication 6

Note From the Author 7

Introduction 8

The Purpose of Life 10

Confidence 14

Beauty 20

Health 24

Energy 26

Memory 29

Patterns 32

Trust  34

Damage Control  37

Compromise  39

Time Management  41

The Shaolin Monk  43

Luck  45

Spirituality  47

Good Versus Evil  49

Depression and Suicide  53

Grief  55

Drugs  58

Rejection  60

Enemies  62

Self Defense  64

Money  67

Greed  69

Youth  71

Hobbies  73

Imagination 76

Humor 78

Hope 80

You're the Hero 81

Question and Answer 82

More Wise Words 88

My Favorite Chinese Proverbs 92

Happiness 96

The Second To Last Word 102

The Truth 104

# Dedication

This book is dedicated to the living, in remembrance of the dead.

# Note From the Author

No one can tell you what's fun and what isn't. If you like something, then you know it, and you go have fun doing it. It's that simple. I put this first and foremost in hope that you never get lost while trying to understand my book.

# Introduction

Your overall outlook on life is important. Negative thoughts are no good unless you use them to make yourself a better person.

Stop the negative thoughts. Happiness is a state of mind. Don't be one of those people who isn't happy even when you get your way.

If you think my book is useless to you, because you are such a loser that there is no hope for you, you need to stop thinking that. Every person who is alive today is having a better life than most creatures that have lived on the Earth. There are so many different animals you could have been born to be, yet you were born to be a human –the top animal. Also there are so many different eras of time you could have been born into, yet you were born into the 20$^{th}$ and 21$^{st}$ centuries and its technology, knowledge, and amusements. You are very, very fortunate to be the person that you are. Don't waste the opportunity you have.

"People are just as happy as they make up their minds to be." –Abraham Lincoln

"The greater part of our happiness or misery depends on our disposition and not our circumstances." –Martha Washington

# The Purpose Of Life

So, what is the meaning of life? Don't worry about the meaning of life and why we're here. It has been established that we don't know. If I had to answer, I'd say there is no meaning of life, and we're here because of evolution (n. the changing of things through time, natural selection, and overall environment). Also don't worry about how the Earth, sun, and universe got here in the first place, okay?

But there is a question that sounds very similar to those, and it is a very important question. What is the PURPOSE of life? Now to answer this question, you have to look at every facet of the big picture that is life. After personally doing this, while understanding limiting factors like time, energy, and death, I have concluded the purpose of life is to have as much happiness and fun as possible, before time runs out and you die.

This seems like a simple concept, but I am amazed by how many people claim to be unhappy, and by people content to choose lives for themselves that are full of stress and chores. Well, we all have to do some chores and stressful activities, but many people seem like they just don't know how to increase their happiness levels.

I would like you to pause for a moment and think of somebody who is no fun at all –not someone you hate, but somebody who is never happy and who doesn't seem like they're making any effort to be happy. Have you decided who that is yet? Good.

If you examine this person for a minute, you will notice negative characteristics. Like, he never wants to do anything, or he works 50 hours a week at a job he can't stand, he doesn't get along with people, or worst of all, he doesn't even want to get along with people. This person is the opposite of who you want to be if you are going to enjoy yourself.

If you couldn't think of anyone for the exercise, then look at Scrooge, the miser with no Christmas spirit. He didn't seem to care about people, and had a big frown. So if you don't want to be like that, then the opposite of this person would be a role model. Yes. To me, the most important factor in deciding that someone is a role model is: this person is having a genuinely great time in general, while staying on the side of good. I explain why it's important to be on the side of good in other parts of this book. While reading this book, I'd like you to keep in mind that "the purpose of your life is to have as much happiness and fun as possible –before time runs out and you die."

# Confidence

Confidence is happening in your subconscious. It is the driving force behind most of what you do, and many of the opinions you have. To break this down for you –a very confident person will naturally speak up in class, ask out a girl he likes, or pursue his dreams, because he believes he's good enough to reach them. Someone who lacks confidence might not naturally speak up in class, might not ask out the girl, and might not pursue his dreams.

Thus, confidence is very important. The huge impact that having confidence makes, means it is a necessity if you're going to have an enjoyable life.

Having an enjoyable life is the point of this book, and the point of living.

Confidence comes from within yourself. People can compliment you all day long, about everything you do, but if you don't believe it, then you're being too hard on yourself. It is good to remain humble on the outside, so people don't mistake you for simply being high on yourself. But you just HAVE to believe in yourself if you expect to achieve happiness. Happiness is not just an achievement. It is the greatest achievement.

Without confidence, you will go through life with a great handicap. The difference between having one leg and lacking confidence is: you can do something about lacking confidence! You can manufacture confidence by overcoming fear and believing in yourself. That statement is the key to gaining confidence.

If you think that you are confident, then great – you have a foundation to build on. If you are not confident, then you need to work on it. Possibly, it's as simple as forcing yourself to have the courage to do things. It will get easier to do something that you're afraid of as you get more practice at it. Don't force too much though, or you won't be happy. The other easiest way to manufacture confidence is to remind yourself often about your very favorite things about yourself... If you don't have any favorite things about yourself, then look harder. There actually are cool things inside of most people.

Because confidence is a subconscious thing, not something you're constantly aware of, people might not even realize that it's confidence that they lack. Having a negative view of the future is a sign of low confidence. It is best to be a realist (n. one who is accurate about their predictions of the future) while working towards making your future brighter.

My best example to explain why a pessimist lacks confidence: A guy in his early 20's who's never had a girlfriend –really worried that he may never find his true love. First of all, today's world has convinced him that he has failed; there are people younger than him who are married or who have kids. (Many of these people have made a mistake that they don't realize until it's too late).

A much better view of this situation calls for confidence. With confidence, he can believe that he is an eligible bachelor, with a lot to offer to one lucky woman. If he somehow really doesn't think he has any positive traits, then he needs to think of some fast. Here are a few positive traits that girls might like: he doesn't have any girl problems at all, past or present –no babies, no diseases, no psycho ex's, and he's a gentleman looking to devote himself to one girl. That short list alone is possibly more than we can say about the girls he likes.

Sometimes people are just plain too hard on themselves, and that alone is ruining their confidence. This is bad. Many of these people are actually achieving, looking good, and winning –but nothing's ever good enough. This will bring your confidence down, and your happiness down. Meanwhile you were actually pretty good. Once again, confidence comes from within you, and is crucial (adj. very important) to gaining the highest achievement: happiness.

The opposite of confidence is fear. To quote Yoda in Star Wars Episode 1: Fear leads to anger. Anger leads to hate. Hate leads to suffering.

"Confidence is the hinge on the door to success." –Mary O'Hare Dumas

"Who has confidence in himself will gain the confidence of others." –Leib Lazarow

"No one can make you feel inferior without your consent." –Eleanor Roosevelt

# Beauty

Beauty is in the eye of the beholder. Although this is true, to me it sounds like a consolation prize – like, well, not everybody thinks that's ugly!

Instead of settling for the honorable mention before you've even lost... Wouldn't it be much better to increase the percentage of beholders that see the beauty in you? This is possible. It just takes a little effort.

She has a great personality! So does Snowball. Call people superficial, but the fact is physical attraction and noticing beauty, almost always starts with a person's appearance. If the girl with the great personality could have made a devotion to losing weight a long time ago, she could have been introduced as "she's pretty hot." She has just gone from fat to low-level heartbreaker by fixing one thing about her appearance.

This said, beauty is skin deep –but ugly goes clean to the bone. Don't underestimate the power and importance of beauty. Being attractive has plenty of advantages.

So, you look good? Great. Just like having confidence, you have a foundation to build on. You don't look so good, you know it, and you wish I would help? Well, there are too many specific things that may need help, to explain each one. Basic rule number one is: if it ain't broke, then don't try and fix it.

If you go to the mirror, you will probably be reminded of what makes you less than gorgeous. If you keep getting this feeling that girls don't like your

Mohawk, then they probably don't. But if you really can't tell what aspect of your beauty could use a little work, ask somebody. Ask a few people separately, even.

This is an important question to you, so don't be too quick to dye your hair blonde because some moron decided that's the answer. Many people find it very easy to help with someone else's physical appearance. In general, people see others much more clearly than they see themselves. If the answer is that your hygiene stinks, then you should realize this yourself, and try to do better. Your friend might be too nice to tell you to take a shower. Also, don't underestimate the importance of good clothes and shoes. Act like you want em, you know what I'm saying?

It's actually all about looking good. Because if you look good, then you feel good. And if you feel good, then you play good.

"Even beauties can be unattractive. If you catch a beauty in the wrong light at the right time, forget it. I believe in low lights and trick mirrors. I believe in plastic surgery." –Andy Warhol

"Vanity is definitely my favorite sin." –John Milton, The Devil's Advocate

# Health

Your health is the number one most important thing you should care about. Being in good health is a great foundation to build on if you want to be happy. It is possible to be happy and not healthy, but it's harder to do.

The systems of the human body need 2 main things for health –oxygen and water. This seems to go without saying, but it is my understanding that most people don't drink enough water, AND they don't breathe right either. Taking slower deeper breaths keeps the body better oxygenated, gives people more energy, and helps the lymph system clean the body of impurities better. Drinking plenty of water helps remove impurities too, and also keeps the body alive in general. Every house should have a water filter and a supply of pure drinking water. Over 90% of the human body is made up of water.

It's best to care about the health of your body every day. Eating right, getting enough sleep, exercising, and avoiding stressful activities will all contribute to a healthy lifestyle. If you take care of your health, other factors that go into being happy should fall into place much easier.

"Be careful when reading health books. You may die of a misprint." –Mark Twain

"Hygiene is two thirds of health." –Lebanese Proverb

# Energy

Some people have more physical energy than others. It seems that if we want to have more energy, there is nothing we can do about it. Having energy to do the things you want to do is important to being happy, so it needs to be mentioned here.

If you have plenty of energy in your life already, then don't let me confuse you. If you don't have plenty of energy, you might want to look at energy as concentration plus enthusiasm. When I break it down like this, it's easier to see what we need to do if we want to have the energy to do something. If you enthusiastically concentrate on something you're doing, you can't possibly be lazy and uninterested. It can be hard to be energetic about something if you don't want to do it, but you can still try to concentrate on it, and try to find something amusing about it.

It's really sad to go through life without any energy, so if this is your situation, it needs to be addressed if you're going to be happy. I would even recommend going out of your way to increase energy levels. Getting more sleep is a great place to start. Quitting drugs, alcohol, or cigarettes will only help. Taking vitamins, eating right, drinking enough water, and breathing right will help your energy levels too. It has also been proven that exercise will lead to increased energy levels.

"Nothing great was ever achieved without enthusiasm." –Ralph Waldo Emerson

"Exercise gives you endorphins. Endorphins make people happy and happy people just don't shoot their husbands. They just don't." –Legally Blonde, Movie

# Memory

This book would be incomplete without mentioning memory. In my opinion, memory is directly proportional to wisdom. What I mean by this is: the larger your collection of valid memory, the wiser you will be.

That's hard for me to explain, but if you look at it on a large scale –if you literally forget everything that ever happens, you're going to be a moron. If you literally remember everything that ever happens, and every story you hear, I promise you'll be pretty wise. For one thing, you can avoid making the same mistakes twice.

So how do you improve your memory? Well, you make an honest effort to remember things. Start by getting enough sleep at night. Take a multivitamin pill every single morning. Sometimes I take extra B complex, vitamin E, vitamin C, or spirulina too.

Also, let events sink in. Don't just move on to the next thing mindlessly. Personally, I look for chances to think about things. At the end of a day is a great time to reflect on the day's events, and the hot topics in your life. I hate the expression "don't think too much."

Finally, I have to add that there's a big difference between intelligence and wisdom. Intelligence consists of mainly trivial knowledge and your capacity for learning more trivial knowledge. Wisdom is the true measuring stick for how smart someone is. When you apply your knowledge of the world towards making correct life decisions, that's when you have wisdom. Never mess with the wise man...

"Knowledge is power." –Francis Bacon

"Knowledge speaks but wisdom listens." –Jimi Hendrix

# Patterns

History repeats itself. This is a very useful statement, but an often misunderstood one. When people think of history, they might think of Hitler and how he ultimately failed. Those that forget history are condemned to repeat it. Well I'm never going to be in a position to take over the world, so yeah, yeah. History repeats itself. Big deal.

You're right. Looking at history on that large a scale can be pretty useless. Now remember those tacos you had last week. You wouldn't want that to repeat! That's what I'm talking about…

The concept of patterns is all about learning from successes and mistakes. The tacos upset your stomach and put you in the bathroom. So you wisely never eat them again. There are patterns to everything, and recognizing them is a big deal.

If you pay enough attention to patterns, you can predict people's reactions better. Learning patterns is a combination of experience plus memory. It goes without saying that if you keep forgetting enough minor experiences, you will be worse at recognizing patterns.

"Don't wait for it to happen. Don't even want it to happen. Just watch what does happen." –Jim Malone, The Untouchables

# Trust

Realizing who not to trust, based on their trust record, is one of the most important patterns to recognize. There are very intelligent people who will even go as far as to say: trust no one. It certainly is a sad state of affairs if you're trying to live happily in a world where you can't trust anybody.

Since the goal is to be happy, I recommend giving people a chance –a chance to be your friend and to enjoy life with you. I also recommend putting educated limits on how far you trust them. Just make sure you realize that anybody can turn on you and burn you at any time.

It is very important to watch who you get involved with. There are so many people who wind up wishing they had never met somebody in their life. And if it does turn out that you make a mistake and someone is a problem in your life, the best thing to do is to try to peacefully get away from that person. Don't go for revenge. Don't carry on about petty amounts of money or items. Simply, don't have anything to do with that person. 99% of the time these tactics will be good enough to make a clean split from knowing somebody. If you have a problem with a true psycho who won't leave you alone and is a threat to physically hurt you, you need to hide far, far away. I can't recommend any other action.

"The best proof of love is trust." –Joyce Brothers

"Few things can help an individual more than to place responsibility on him, and to let him know that you trust him." –Booker T. Washington, Up From Slavery

"If someone betrays you once it is their fault. If someone betrays you twice it is your fault." –Eleanor Roosevelt

"Trust, but verify." –Ronald Reagan

# Damage Control

When something isn't going well, it's best to recognize that it isn't going well. The sooner you recognize that there's a problem, the quicker you can start trying to fix the problem. One way I can help you understand this better is to apply this to relationships. It happens over and over and over again that people stick around somebody until there's a major problem, when they knew all along that this person was trouble. Usually there are plenty of signs that you shouldn't be spending time with somebody, before that person turns against you.

Damage control isn't only about relationships. I was just using that as an example. Damage control is about noticing that something isn't going right, and trying to fix it by examining your options. Once something goes terribly wrong is no time to say "gee, uh. Maybe I shouldn't have done that." People in general are terrible at predicting the future. You will be way ahead of the game if you apply your wisdom, and knowledge of history and patterns, towards predicting the future of your actions. Think baby! Life is a thinking man's game...

"You gonna do something, or just stand there and bleed?" –Wyatt Earp, Tombstone

# Compromise

Any healthy relationship has a foundation of compromise. What you want and what your friend, lover, or family member wants can be two different things. Neither side should attempt to have too much control in a relationship. If you want to watch your relationships fall apart, then try forcing your wishes on people.

I'd say that if you save your demands for when it's really, really important, you'll have a much better chance of getting what you want. Once again, to some of us this whole concept of compromise seems basic, but we all know people who need a lesson in compromise. There are a lot of hot-headed people out there, with strong opinions –and in the end, both them and their friends suffer because of the lack of compromise.

My advice is to point it out to somebody that they are terrible at compromising, if you care about that person. It's very constructive criticism. Tell that person "I've never seen you compromise anything in your entire life" if it's that bad. Seriously. Because if that person continues to make demands on you, you're going to be unhappy –until eventually the relationship ends in a grand finale of unhappiness.

I suggest that you take a look at yourself for a minute. Are you one of those people who can't compromise? Now is your chance to realize it before you lose any more friends.

# Time Management

Understanding time management is one of the keys to good life. Unfortunately, it is not obvious what we should be doing with our time, if we want to use our time perfectly. So I try to just do my best. To me, it's a matter of prioritizing. It's about having my priorities straight. Basically, I rate everything's importance. Then I do the thing with the highest importance rating.

I share your concern for not having enough time. Another thing I do is I try to do everything fast.

If I catch myself being slow, I try to pick up the pace – thus manufacturing small amounts of time for other things.

"This is your life, and it's ending one minute at a time." –Narrator, Fight Club

"Time is money." –Benjamin Franklin, Advice to a Young Tradesman

"It takes less time to do a thing right than it does to explain why you did it wrong." – Henry Wadsworth Longfellow

# The Shaolin Monk

I admit that I don't know much about the Shaolin monk. Even after watching a Jet Li movie and reading more about the monks, there is plenty that I don't know about how they live their lives. Though, I do know that some of the basic attitudes that they have, make them into very strong people.

As I learned about the monks, it seemed clear why the monks were so good at fighting and martial arts. They practiced intensely –fast, for many hours, and without losing concentration. I was amazed at the way they saw things like eating to be a waste of time. The movie showed the monks eating a meal together –they practically shoveled it down their throats!

Time is the great limiting factor. To truly understand this can actually add days, even years to your life.

# Luck

I've been studying to be the luckiest person in the world. There's a formula for luck. It's preparation plus opportunity.

It's real simple. Situations and opportunities will come up, and the more prepared you are for them, the luckier you're going to seem. That's all you need to know about luck, but don't take it for granted.

"I find that the harder I work, the more luck I have." –Thomas Jefferson

"Let your hook be always cast. In the pool where you least expect it, will be fish." –Ovid (For example, if you dress well every time you leave your house, you will be dressed well when you see the girl of your dreams.)

"Luck is infatuated with the efficient." –Persian Proverb

# Spirituality

It's possible there is no God or spirits.  Maybe everything is all cut and dry and we evolved from cave men naturally through evolution.  We will never know for sure what the truth is.  If you believe in a religion though, then I encourage you to continue believing.

For one thing, believing in a God will help keep you honest, and nice, and out of trouble.  It's very easy to get in trouble in this world, especially considering you only get one chance.  Our bodies are going to be dead for billions and billions of years.  I think that we may as well behave ourselves, and hope for the chance that we have some kind of soul or spirit. I mean, it would be kind of a disaster if you act evil in this short life, and then pay for it eternally.

The point is there are multiple reasons why we should behave ourselves, and the slight possibility of eternal punishment is one of them.

"If men are so wicked with religion, what would they be without it?" –Ben Franklin

# Good Versus Evil

This world is sick. Through evolution, people have become bigger, faster, and smarter. Some people don't accept that people are smarter now than 100 or 1000 years ago, but it's true. To confirm this for you, look at this on a large scale and compare yourself to a Neanderthal (n. pre-historic man).

More and more people are becoming sick in the head as time goes on, in all sorts of ways. Also, more and more people are becoming secretly evil, for their own personal pleasure. The great decline in basic morals is obvious. The United States, at least, is already a state of people, each out for themselves, making sure to never admit it.

I consider a safe level of paranoia to be a good idea. It's called watching your back. There is no use in ignoring this situation. If you want to act oblivious, the target sign on you will grow.

So wait. You're confused. I defined a role model as a person who is having a genuinely great time in general, while staying on the side of good. Now, wouldn't you be happier if you do what makes you feel good, even if it is immoral?

Well, yeah. You would be happier sometimes. Living for the moment in immoral ways can wind up making you unhappy in the end, though. Part of taking care of your health involves staying out of trouble with people and the law. And this is the main reason why I encourage people to be good. Evil people are almost always unhappy for most of their lives, or unhappy in the end. Ever hear of jail, murder, or revenge? Since this book is called How To

Be Happy, I can't just sit here and let you be evil, if it's going to make you unhappy!

But why is it so important to me to be on the side of good? Besides the fact that being evil will get you in serious trouble... We have the gift of life for a very short time. I, for one, have to respect the length of eternal death –and hope for the chance there is an afterlife, as improbable as it may seem.

It took me a while to figure this out –I guess no one ever told it to me like that. It seemed like there were different religions with different beliefs... and you may as well just go for yours and hope for the best. I stole, lied, and did things I wasn't allowed to. I got caught a few times, and wound up in some unhappy situations.

Nowadays, I behave myself. Often I wear the Medallion of Miracles around my neck. To me it means Under God. I also use it to remind myself to be honest always. These actions, plus a good deed here and there, are my personal appeal to God –in hope that He's really out there somewhere… because eternity is an awfully long time.

"Honesty is the first chapter in the book of wisdom." –Thomas Jefferson

"We ARE the people our parents warned us about." –Jimmy Buffet

"Darkness cannot drive out darkness. Only light can do that. Hate cannot drive out hate. Only love can do that." –Martin Luther King Jr.

# Depression and Suicide

Five billion years went by to get to this one point in time where you've got life –and then you're going to be dead for infinity. Don't gloss over that. Read it again. You've got this one little point in time where you have life. Don't waste it.

That should pretty much convince you that you want to be alive. I remind everyone I know of these facts when they get down on their lives.

I think there is such a thing as clinical depression –but I think it's rare. Most of you are just head cases.  What I mean by head cases is –you don't need pills, you need to change some of your opinions and hang-ups.  Hopefully, you can find one or two rays of hope in this book.

You don't want to die. So sit down and shut up.


"Be happy while you're living, for you're a long time dead." –Scottish Proverb

"Don't let life discourage you.  Everyone who got where he is, had to begin where he was." – Richard Evans

"You can complain because roses have thorns, or you can rejoice because thorns have roses." –Ziggy

"Until you value yourself, you won't value your time.  Until you value your time, you will not do anything with it." –M Scott Peck

# Grief

I really hate the word grief for some reason. I don't know why I hate hearing somebody talk about grief, but when I think of grief, I think of somebody wasting precious time, life force, energy, etc. because of their mental hang-ups. Don't get me wrong – losing someone you care about is a horrible thing. I've had people I loved die suddenly and without warning, and it definitely gives you hours of unhappy thoughts, no matter what strategy you try to use to fight it.

Actually there were 3 different people in my life who died suddenly and without warning –my mom and sister died when I was 19, and my best friend died when I was 16. And I know what the answer to grief is. The answer is to not become another victim of the tragic death of your loved one. The person who you loved may be gone, but you're still here. That person doesn't want you to be in mourning for too long. I mean, the sadness of the death will never disappear completely, but you both know that you loved each other, and you don't have to go about your life trying to keep proving it to yourself. Your loved one wants you to be happy! Even if it means not grieving over the death! It may be hard, but the healthiest way to handle the death is to cherish the beautiful memories, and accept that which we can not change.

Put the memories in your heart and go on with a new appreciation of life. The most positive way I used the deaths of the people I loved was to go on trying to be someone who they could be proud of.

"We should try never to let our happy frame of mind be disturbed.  Whether we are suffering at present or have suffered in the past, there is no reason to be unhappy.  If we can remedy it, why be unhappy?  And if we cannot, what use is there in being depressed about it?  That just adds more unhappiness and does no good at all." –the 14th Dalai Lama, Tenzin Gyatso

# Drugs

Good drugs and the right video games are the cornerstones of a great life. Just joking. I'm telling you; don't even experiment with hard drugs. Recreational use of pot is OK in moderation. A little bit of drinking can be fun too, but I guess you already know that.

No, there's something about hard drugs, that some people get addicted and totally lost in them. As for just trying drugs a few times, later in life when you get more health-conscious, you'll regret it. My advice is, try your best not to need substances to have a good time. Do you remember the true stories you heard about people who had everything to live for, but couldn't beat their drug addiction? You know you don't want to wind up like that.

"To cease smoking is the easiest thing I ever did. I ought to know. I've done it a thousand times."
–Mark Twain

# Rejection

Any girl that doesn't want to go out with me... doesn't have to go out with me. No anger. No jealousy. She may have even done me a major favor by going away. There's no use in thinking about it too much, unless I'm going to try to learn something.

I look around me and I see all kinds of cornballs with cool girlfriends. So there's hope for you if you're lame. I'd say that if you keep trying to meet women, eventually one of them will love you. Meeting someone who loves you is about the law of percentages –even if most people find you annoying, there will eventually be somebody who loves you. You just have to keep trying to meet people if you're looking for love, and use rejection as simply a learning experience.

Being rejected by family, groups of people, or former friends is harder to deal with. Basically, you want to try to not wind up in that position in the first place. If it happens… learn from it and become stronger!

`"The lady doth protest too much, methinks." – William Shakespeare, Hamlet: Act 3, Scene 2

"I wish they would only take me as I am." – Vincent Van Gogh, Dear Theo: Autobiography of Vincent Van Gogh

"A successful person is one who can lay a firm foundation with the bricks that others throw at him." –David Brink

# Enemies

There is no percentage in pissing people off. Especially since you're so important, and most other people are irrelevant –when it all comes down to it. If someone shoots you, you lose your life. Does it really matter what happens to the person who shot you? Not really.

You have to value your life before you can appreciate what I'm saying. Basically, yeah, I do recommend letting things slide. Getting arrested for hurting someone is very bad –and getting retaliated on by someone is very bad. Sitting there and slowly calming down is your best option.

Be careful. As far as we know, we only get one little life. These people who you don't like are irrelevant, and they are going to have problems in their lives, whether you give it to them or not!

I'm kind of joking, but imagine that every male around you is a 300 pound killer. That's what I do, mainly because I don't approve of picking on the weak either. Picking on the weak doesn't make you look cool, believe it or not. And there's nothing worse than underestimating somebody. Always give people more credit than they deserve, and you will barely ever get burned.

"I treat every man as a gentleman, not because he is, but because I am." –Ben Franklin

"When anger rises, think of the consequences." –Confucius

# Self Defense

I don't recommend getting into fights with people because you don't want to get hurt, and you don't want to have enemies either. But if the situation comes up that someone is trying to hurt you, or physically manipulate you, then you will be much better off if you're ready to defend yourself. Whether you're male or female, you should have a few moves ready, and a basic idea of what strategy you would use to physically defend yourself. During a fight is no time to figure this out.

There are many techniques to defend yourself, but the key is to use your brain. The US Marines have a motto, "the warrior's best weapon is his mind." The right mental decisions can change the outcome of a fight.  Think fast and be decisive.  A moment's hesitation can make you a victim.

I'd say that step one should be trying to avoid the fight altogether.  If you're having trouble with that, then you have to look at who the opponent is.  I mean if it's a group of thugs and you're alone, then there is no use trying to be a superhero.  Make a decision and then commit to it.

Also, be careful where you go, and who you deal with.  The people who live the craziest lives, and who stay out all night, almost always have problems eventually.  You think you know this?  Almost everyone around me has negative issues in their lives, which could have been avoided if they "would have just stayed home that night."  I have it burned into the front of my brain that there are no do-overs in this life. There is no reset button for you to erase a disaster.

# Money

Money is fairly important to gaining happiness. I don't understand people who don't agree. Your overall health is always the most important thing. The less health you have, the less hope you're going to have in general. The next most important things after health are happiness and love.

With money, you will be able to take care of your health better, buy material things that make you happy, and become more appealing to the opposite sex. I put it like this: The more money you have, the more tokens you have –in the arcade that is life.

I can't tell you how you can get rich here. How to get money varies from person to person. Also, you don't have to get a ton of money. If you devote your life to making money, you won't have time to enjoy yourself.

"Success usually comes to those who are too busy to be looking for it." –Henry David Thoreau

"A fool and his money are soon parted." – Thomas Tusser, Five Hundred Points of Good Husbandry

"There's no reason to be the richest man in the cemetery. You can't do any business from there." – Colonel Sanders

"Don't stay in bed… Unless you can make money in bed." –George Burns

# Greed

Greed is a very bad thing and it's not always easy to recognize when you're being greedy. There have been many great minds throughout time who have become rich or powerful, and so many of them turned into megalomaniacs. It seems to me that it is human nature to be recklessly greedy. All we can really do is be careful of what we're doing at all times.

Having too much of a good thing usually has nothing to do with being greedy. But if you're getting away with doing something illegal, for example, watch out. If you push your luck too far, you can wind up with major problems.

There are many fun things in life, but many of them should be enjoyed in moderation. Moderation means: not excessive, but not too little either.

"Happiness is not having what you want, but wanting what you have." –Rabbi H. Schachtel, The Real Enjoyment of Living

"If your desires be endless, your cares and fears will be so too." –Thomas Fuller

"Let me tell you Cassius, you yourself are much condemned to have an itching palm. To sell and mart your offices for gold." –William Shakespeare, Julius Caesar Act 4 Scene 3

# Youth

Youth blows right past us. Life feels like it's going to be a long, long time when we're young. Since our minds haven't fully matured when we're kids, it's possible to make mistakes that ruin our whole lives.

If you're 21 or younger and reading this, I'm telling you to be real careful about the decisions you make. There are so many ways to die or ruin your whole life. Please give yourself a fair chance to grow up, because then your mind will be ready for decisions like: should I get pregnant? And should I eat these drugs? Calculate your moves, kid.

Do enjoy every minute of childhood though, if possible. I recommend stopping and thinking frequently. Make sure you're taking it all in. These will be the memories that you bring with you through life, so I'd try to make them good.

"It's never too late to have a happy childhood."
–Tom Robbins, Still Life With Woodpecker

To educate a man in mind and not in morals is to educate a menace to society. –Theodore Roosevelt

# Hobbies

There are many things to do on this planet, so find a few interests! In my opinion, the people who have some random interests are the ones who have more complete lives. I have a friend who is living a fairly complete and happy life. His hobbies include computers, music, snowboarding, video games, spending time with his girlfriend, being social, recording video, and more. He doesn't have time for more hobbies than that, or he would have more hobbies!

I'm the same way. I like playing guitar, DJing, singing, computers, playing football, playing baseball, video games, writing, collecting things, and more.

Even if you took all of these things away from me, I'd still find something to get interested in. My friend and I are never bored in our lives.

But I am amazed at the intelligent people around me who don't know what they should do with their time. There's a lot of this going on, everywhere I look. I suppose that if you WANTED to make baseball your hobby, you would have already done so. I realize this. I have observed many people now, and I'd have to say that many of you need to get interested in at least 2 new things. I'm not suggesting that you force anything upon yourself. I do realize though, that there are so many different things to get involved with, that there are multiple fun hobbies for everybody.

Make the most out of the short time that you have your life. I can't stress this enough. Only you know what's fun for you. If you like something, then you know it, and you go have fun doing it. It's that simple.

"The whole secret of life is to be interested in one thing profoundly and in a thousand things well." –Horace Walpole

"Action may not always bring happiness, but there is no happiness without action." –Benjamin Disraeli

# Imagination

Everyone who is alive has an imagination. It's one thing that can't be taken away from you. It doesn't matter if you're in jail, in a wheelchair, or just ugly –inside your head you can think anything you want.

Using your imagination is not necessary to have a complete and happy life. If you do like to dream, you should still stay in reality. If you choose to make yourself happy by using your imagination, the best time to do it is with your eyes shut right before you fall asleep at night. Having your own imaginary world on the side isn't such a bad thing, especially if it's intense.

"A man's dreams are an index to his greatness." –Zadok Rabinwitz

"Anyone can escape into sleep. We are all geniuses when we dream. The butcher is the poet's equal there." –E. M. Cioran, The Temptation to Exist

"You are what your deep driving desire is. As your desire is, so is your will. As your will is, so is your deed. As your deed is, so is your destiny." – Brihadaranyaka Upanishad

# Humor

Finding things to laugh about will make you happier in your life. What I mean is that I encourage you to try to find things that make you laugh. One of the easiest ways to accomplish this is to make time for a funny TV show or a funny movie. People waste a lot of time that they could have spent laughing. You would laugh a lot more if you made more time for fun and funny activities.

I'd say that the main opponent of laughter is having mental hang-ups. Dwelling on things in the past that you can't change, and letting minor events weigh on your mind are unnecessary. It's tragic if your mind is playing tricks on you so that you can't laugh at life. My best advice is to realize when an event can't be changed and to move on. I think it's also important to realize when you are stressing something that is minor, so you can stop stressing it. It's much easier to laugh and be happy when there aren't negative things weighing down your mind.

"The human race has one really effective weapon, and that is laughter." –Mark Twain

"The most wasted day of all is that during which we have not laughed." –Sebastian Chamfort

"I don't make jokes. I just watch the government and report the facts." –Will Rogers

"All I need to make a comedy is a park, a policeman, and a pretty girl." –Charlie Chaplin

"Blessed is he who has learned to laugh at himself, for he shall never cease to be entertained." – John Powell

# Hope

We have more hope than we realize. As long as you aren't sick and dying, there is plenty of hope for you to improve your life. The key is to not give up, to lose the pessimist thoughts, and to care more about life. Focus on improving the most negative things in your life. Realizing that there is hope for a better future will make you happier, but you have to make the commitment to work for it. Some people seem to be born to be happy, but the rest of us have to earn happiness through effort.

"He who does not hope to win has already lost." –Jose Joaquin Olmedo

# You're the Hero

Consider yourself "the hero of the story" as you walk through life. The story is still being written as long as you're alive. As the hero of the story, there are people looking up to you, waiting for you to show why you are great. You don't want to let your fans down, right? We all have it in us to be a little bit better than we were yesterday.

# Question And Answer

Q: Are you happy?

A: Yes I'm happy. That would be pretty lame if I wasn't happy and I wrote a book about how to be happy! I've had many unhappy things come into my life including untimely deaths of people I love and even homelessness. Yet I have overcome them to find true happiness. This book is an attempt to explain my philosophy, in an effort to help other people become happier in their lives.

Q: A lot of what you say seems like common knowledge to me. Do you realize this?
A: This book is written for everybody, literally. I want everybody from the biggest idiot to the wisest person to be able to read this book and be able to find something that helps them to become happier. I look around me and I see very few people who are completely happy. If you take these comments that you are calling common knowledge, think about them, and try to apply them to yourself, you will be much better off than if you just dismiss my words and say you know it already. If you know it all already, why aren't you as happy as I am?

Q: How long did it take for you to write this book?
A: This book wasn't hurried at all. I wrote this book over the course of 4 years. I didn't want to be responsible for giving bad advice, and I didn't want

to look back and wish I had written a much different book. A book that teaches people how to be happy can never be perfect, but I did my best.

Q: How come you don't have a chapter called Love?
A: I would have, but I think I wrote enough about how to be happy without writing a chapter called Love. I don't really feel comfortable trying to draw up a universal code for love, the way I wrote about everything else in this book. It's not necessary for me to either, although I discussed a few important aspects of love in different chapters. I didn't write this book so I can babble. My intentions were that every sentence of this book be relevant towards helping you become happier. Things like happiness and love are ultimate goals, not methods.

Q: Is it bad to get upset at somebody? Does it bring me down if someone bothers me, or is it OK to get into a minor fight?

A: I'd say you're better off never fighting with anybody. You are very, very important to yourself, and the person who you're getting upset with is probably irrelevant. Some people are crazy and will do something to hurt you, and it's best not to take any chances. Definitely don't fight with people just because you think they're annoying. Instead of hurting someone I don't like, I can usually look critically at that person and see glaring negatives that make me feel a lot better –because the person is usually a loser even if I don't punch him in the face.

Q: IF there's a God, do you really think He would judge us? People are genetically born to be good or bad. Is it really fair that someone is born to be evil and unhappy, and then they get banished to hell when they die???

A: You're right. I don't look at it in terms of heaven and hell though. No one has any idea what really happens when we die, if we have a soul, or if there is a God. I'm looking at the situation based on 2 things: 1) We have one life to live, and eternal death is a very long time, and 2) If there is a God or a spirit world, it is definitely in your best interest to appeal to it –that your soul is positive and good. Do you have no respect for the fact that you're going to be dead for billions of years?!!

Q: It's comments like that one, that make me less happy than I was before. Do you really think it's going to make me happier if you keep talking about death?

A: First of all, I don't "keep talking about death." This book is clearly about life. But death IS a part of life. The sooner we accept what death is, the sooner we will seize the day, and find a new thirst for life. Yes, ignorance is bliss –but to me life is all about being happy, healthy, and wise. See, I'm not content to just make you feel happy. I'm trying to bring people to a higher level of happiness.

# More Wise Words

Actions speak louder than words. –Me

People don't always say what they're thinking. –Me

If someone does you a favor, look for a chance to return the favor... Try not to need too many favors from people. –Me

If it came to you too easy, there's probably a reason why. –Me

If you have to ask for respect, you already have a problem. If you demand respect, then you suck. –Me

If you want something done right, do it yourself. –Me

You must be the change you wish to see in the world. –Mahatma Gandhi

You may delay. But time will not. –Benjamin Franklin

To be completely honest with oneself is the very best effort a human being can make. –Sigmund Freud

Best men are often molded after faults. –William Shakespeare

Time goes by so fast; people go in and out of your life. You must never miss the opportunity to tell these people how much they mean to you. –Cheers

Heaven has no rage like love to hatred turned. Nor hell a fury like a woman scorned. –William Congreve, The Mourning Bride

Believe half of what you see and nothing of what you hear. –Laura F.

Eliminate the impossible and whatever remains, however improbable, must be the truth. – Sherlock Holmes

There is nothing to fear, but fear itself. – Franklin D. Roosevelt, First Inaugural Address

No matter what goes wrong, it will probably look right. –Scott's First Law

If someone offers you a breath mint, accept it. – H. Jackson Brown Jr., Life's Little Treasure Book

In Genesis, it says that it is not good for a man to be alone.  But sometimes it is a great relief. –John Barrymore

It is good to vary in order that you may frustrate the curious, especially those who envy you. –Baltasar Gracian

Loose lips sink ships. (Watch what you say.) – My mother

A good plan today is better than a perfect plan tomorrow. –Conrad Brean, Wag the Dog

Anything that is too stupid to be spoken is sung. –Voltaire

A new commandment I give unto you, that ye love one another. –Jesus

Never let the weeds get higher than the garden. –Tom Waits

The greatest thing in the world is not so much where we are, but in what direction we are moving. –Oliver Wendell Holmes

Always go to the bathroom when you have a chance. –King George the Fifth

# My Favorite Chinese Proverbs

Teachers open the door, but you must enter by yourself.

If you are patient in one moment of anger, you will escape a hundred days of sorrow.

A journey of a thousand miles begins with a single step.

Govern a family as you would cook a small fish –very gently.

You won't help shoots grow by pulling them up higher.

Man who waits for roast duck to fly into mouth must wait very, very long time.

Clear conscience never fears midnight knocking.

He who asks a question is a fool for five minutes.  He who does not ask a question remains a fool forever.

Enough shovels of earth, a mountain.  Enough pails of water, a river.

Of all the stratagems, to know when to quit is the best.

Give a man a fish and he will eat for a day.  Teach a man to fish and he will eat for the rest of his life.

With time and patience, the mulberry leaf becomes a silk gown.

One never needs their humor as much as when they argue with a fool.

Better a diamond with a flaw than a pebble without one.

If you suspect a man, don't employ him. And if you employ him, don't suspect him.

A gem cannot be polished without friction, nor a man perfected without trials.

Never do anything standing that you can do sitting, or anything sitting that you can do lying down.

Sour, sweet, bitter, pungent, all must be tasted.

Those who have free seats at a play, boo first.

Even a rabbit will bite when it is cornered.

Judge not the horse by his saddle.

Make happy those who are near, and those who are far will come.

Keep your broken arm inside your sleeve.

One should be just as careful in choosing one's pleasures as in avoiding calamities.

A fall into a ditch makes you wiser.

Dream different dreams while on the same bed.

With true friends, even water drunk together is sweet enough.

An ant may well destroy a whole dam.

A sly rabbit will have three openings to its den.

To know the road ahead, ask those coming back.

It is later than you think.

Assess the advantages in taking advice, then structure your forces accordingly, to supplement extraordinary tactics. Forces are to be structured strategically, based on what is advantageous. Sun Tzu - The Art of War.

# Happiness

## By: Daimion Cadet

What is happiness? As humans, we play with different ideas of what happiness is. Sometimes we try to find happiness with material things and endless sexual partners. For the most part we are in denial; staying in bad relationships, in hopes that we will be happy in the long run, or that the partner that we are with will change to be the perfect person we want them to be. Let's keep it real –if the person you are with is a schmuck when you first meet them, 9 out of 10 times they will be a schmuck in the end. To understand what happiness is, we have to look within ourselves.

How can we enjoy life, or understand the meaning of happiness, if we don't look at what is going on inside ourselves first? How can one share or promote happiness if we ourselves aren't happy? So let's ask that lingering question: What is happiness, and how do we obtain it? For the most part the answer is right in front of us. People come with a lot of baggage, both emotional and physical. Sometimes it's not even our own fault. So if you're someone who had a normal upbringing, with no sexual and mental abuse, there is hope for you. Ask yourself this simple question: what makes you happy?

Take a minute or an hour to really answer that question. Sit back, look at your life from the outside, analyze your current situations, and see what you come up with. The answer is usually in front of you, but for the most part we don't like the outcome of our findings. If getting rid of that loser you're with will help you obtain happiness, then do it. Don't be afraid to be by yourself. We all need to be by ourselves from time to time. Jumping from relationship to relationship without any healing time is unhealthy, and adds to unhappiness.

    Many people have come to the conclusion that money and power is the true meaning of happiness, but we see time and time again that isn't so. It doesn't hurt to have money and power. It does help make things better, but then we worry whether or not the person we are with is here for our money or us. With all these situations that pop up, how are we supposed to turn out normal? Being rich doesn't make us happy, being poor is a bitch at times. So what is the answer?

How the hell am I supposed to know; I am searching for the same thing! Seriously, I found out the answer, and I think most of you can relate to what I'm about to say. One day I sat down and took a good look at my life. Things weren't going the way I had dreamed. I was changing women like I change underwear, and I had no significant other in my life. I didn't have a job, and the pot I had to piss in was getting smaller. I thought about ending it all a couple of times and when I thought I hit rock bottom, the key to my happiness suddenly came to me. I decided to count my blessings instead of dwelling on my negatives. I realized that I was fortunate to be healthy and to have a good head on my shoulders. And other than bills, there wasn't really too much stress on me.

Women and men come and go. So basically what I'm saying is: happiness comes from within. Take time to look at your life and clean house, and get rid of all the negative things around you, may it be people, places, or things. Be brave. You know what you want, so do what you know is best for you. Get rid of your mental crutches. Its not going to be easy – nothing you really want ever is.

Let's break it down a little further. What types of concerns keep you from being happy? You may be short, fat, not down with the in crowd, too tall, or have something else that you're not satisfied with. The truth of the matter is that someone you think looks perfect, probably has plenty of problems. It takes a lot of hard work to be so-called perfect. It takes a lot to eat and then go and throw up. Being perfect really isn't all that perfect. So before you go out and envy the next person, think about what it took for them to look the way they do. Many people think of happiness as outer beauty. In today's society we can't help but have that state of mind, because every time we look around we see an ad with someone who looks great, has a nice body, and not an inch of fat.

Put down that extra piece of donut if you don't like the way you look, because exercising isn't easy. And don't give up on something, just because it's hard. It's like the old saying –once you fall off a horse you need to get back on; no pain no gain. Happiness is similar, in that we have to earn it. We all know deep inside what it would take to make us happy; it's all about taking that extra step to make it happen. I'm not talking about a drastic step like getting liposuction, or taking out a second mortgage to get plastic surgery, just take it one day at a time.

# The Second To Last Word

## By: Sammy Divella

My Aunt Josephine, the wisest woman I know, has always told me that nothing and nobody will make me completely happy unless I am happy and content with myself first. I totally agree. If you are happy and content with yourself first, and then you become rich or find the love of your life, well that's just icing on the cake.

I believe the three main things you need to work on in order to be happy are self-esteem, motivation, and determination. My favorite quote of all time is from Mel Gibson in the movie Braveheart. "Every man dies, not every man really lives." That goes for everybody, not just men. Thinking about that quote, I don't want to die unless I really live well and to the fullest. The bottom line is, give positive energy and you will receive positive feedback. If you put out negative energy and vibes, and you are a miserable bastard, then you will always receive negative feedback, and you will be a miserable bastard for the rest of your life. Just be happy!

# The Truth

## By: Jason J. Hendrickson

The truth is like a rock,
It can't be bent or twisted.
The truth can be chiseled,
Made into true beauty.

The truth flows like birds in a flock,
One wrong turn and you missed it.
The truth comes secret and answers riddled,
Peace from the comforter to protect eternity.